Sporran Explains Highland Games

Linda J. Purves

illustrated by Michael Musgrove

AuthorHouse™ UK Ltd.
500 Avebury Boulevard
Central Milton Keynes, MK9 2BE
www.authorhouse.co.uk
Phone: 08001974150

© 2008 Linda J. Purves. All rights reserved.

No part of this book may be reproduced, stored in a retrieval system, or transmitted by any means without the written permission of the author.

First published by AuthorHouse 7/3/2008

ISBN: 978-1-4343-4553-0 (sc)

Printed in the United States of America
Bloomington, Indiana

This book is printed on acid-free paper.

Hello! My name is Sporran and I'm a Highland Pony.
I live in the Scottish Highlands and every summer I like to visit Highland Games.
Let me tell you all about them...

Highland Games began hundreds of years ago. The head of each clan, called the chieftain, held gatherings to help him find his best men to go with him into battle. Running and jumping competitions tested speed and agility. Hill races tested endurance, and heavy lifting contests tested strength.

Only the fittest, fastest, and strongest men would be chosen as the chieftain's soldiers.

The competitors could win prizes of gold coins or special swords but most of the men competed for the honour of being considered the best.

In those days, messengers had to run on foot across steep and boggy ground to spread any news. The chieftain often needed to send out speedy messages to his clan when he wanted them to gather for battle. Hill races helped him find his best men for the task.

Nowadays, spectators come from all over the world to see dancers dance the Highland Fling and hear pipers play the bagpipes as they watch the Highland Games.

Men used to dance the Highland Fling on top of their leather shields placed on the ground. Competitors must still perform the dance on the spot.

One legend says that the Highland Fling is the dancer imitating a stag, with arms and hands in the air like the stag's antlers.

There are competitions for pipe bands and also for solo pipers.

It's summertime in Scotland
Off to the Games we go
Picnic basket at the ready
Looking forward to the show

See the dancers and the pipers
On the stage now specially built
Is she dancing the Highland Fling
Or are there midges in her kilt?

Tossing The Caber

The caber is a big, heavy wooden log. It is about 18 feet (5.5 metres) long and weighs about 150 lbs (68 kilograms).

One end of the caber is thicker than the other and the competitor begins with the thick end resting on his shoulder. He then moves along the caber until he can get his hands under the thin end. He balances the caber up straight and then runs a few steps before he tosses it up in the air.

To win the caber tossing competition, he must try to get his caber to flip over and land on the ground in a straight line. The judge stands behind the competitor when he tosses the caber and then imagines they are standing inside a clock face. The winner will be the competitor who flips the caber to land closest to the twelve o'clock position.

Each venue has its own caber but it is difficult to keep the caber at exactly the same weight each year as the wood dries out making it lighter.

Sometimes the caber is soaked in a river before the Games to make sure it is heavy enough.

In the Guinness Book Of Records, the biggest caber ever recorded was 25 feet (7.62 metres) long and weighed 280 lbs (127 kilograms).

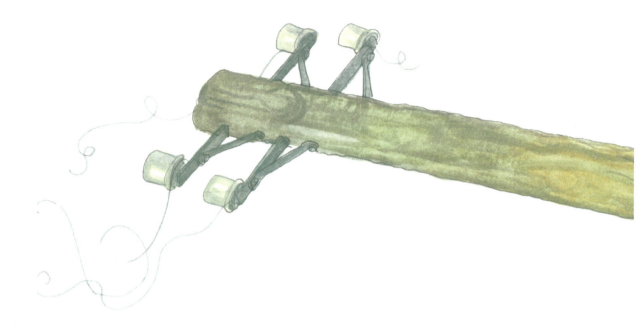

Breakfast starts a Scotsman's day
Heaps of porridge in his bowl
Now he's feeling super strong
He might toss a telegraph pole!

The Shot

The shot is an iron ball which weighs 16 lbs (7.27 kilograms) or 22 lbs (10 kilograms).
The competitor is allowed a short run up to a wooden marker on the ground called a trig. From the trig he must throw the shot from in front of his shoulder with only one hand.

In the old days, the shot would have been a smooth stone from the local river.

To win the competition, he must throw the shot the longest distance.

The Scottish record for throwing the 22 lbs (10 kilograms) shot is 53 feet 4 inches (around 16 metres).

The Scottish record for throwing the 16 lbs (7.27 kilograms) shot is 65 feet 3 inches (around 20 metres).

With weight upon his shoulder
To throw the furthest he must try
But what's this? It's not a stone
He's throwing a Scotch pie!

Throwing The Hammer

The Scots Hammer is an iron ball on a special handle called a shaft. It is 4 feet 2 inches (1.27 metres) long and can weigh 16 lbs (7.27 kilograms) or 22 lbs (10 kilograms).

The competitor stands with his back to a wooden marker on the ground called a trig. He lifts the hammer to swing it once around over his head and then throws it over his shoulder.

To win the hammer throwing competition he must through the hammer the longest distance.

Competitors wear special boots with spikes in the toes to give them extra grip.

In the old days, the Scots Hammer would have been the local blacksmith's sledgehammer.

The Scottish record for the 16 lbs (7.27 kilograms) hammer throw is 156 feet 8.5 inches (around 48 metres).

The Scottish record for the 22 lbs (10 kilograms) hammer throw is 129 feet 10.5 inches (around 40 metres).

Lift it high and over head
Swing it round is what he'll do
Not looking where he's throwing
Watch out! In the porta-loo

Throwing The Weight

There are two different competitions for throwing the weight. One is to throw the weight the furthest and the other is to throw the weight the highest.

Furthest

The weight is a ball on a chain with a handle and weighs 28 lbs
(12.7 kilograms).
The competitor holds the weight in one hand and lifts it
up to swing it around behind him. He then spins
himself and the weight around three times, as if dancing a waltz.
On the third swing, he lets go of the weight to throw it as far as he can.

Sometimes the thrower gets dizzy and lets go at the wrong time. A net safety cage is used to catch the weight if it goes in the wrong direction.

Highest

The weight is shaped like a box with a ring handle on the top and weighs 56 lbs (24.5 kilograms).
A bar is raised up between two posts and the competitor has three attempts to throw the weight over the bar using only one hand. The bar goes higher and higher to find the winner.

There are always plenty of spare bars available as the weight often breaks the bar on the way back down.

Some competitors swing the weight low between their legs before throwing it high in the air.

A Scotsman swings up to the trig
Hundreds watching, feeling shy
A gust of wind, oh! what a shock
His kilt's been lifted high

Tug O' War

Tug O' War teams can be made up of five or eight members plus one coach. The teams pick up the rope and the centre is then marked on the ground with a flag. The rope is also marked 6 feet (1.8 metres) from the centre on each side. The aim is to pull the rope marker of the other team over the centre flag. Teams change ends after round one and it's the best of three to find the winners.

The coach walks up and down alongside his team to shout encouragement.

Some rounds last as long as twenty minutes with both teams hardly moving!

Haste ye back!

Printed in the United States
1299LVUK00002B